# On Care to Be Had for the Dead

# On Care to Be Had for the Dead

## St. Augustine

# On Care to Be Had for the Dead

© Lighthouse Publishing 2017

Written by: St. Augustine (Nov.13 354 – Aug.28 430)

Translated by: Rev. H. Browne, M.A.

Updated into Modern U.S English by A.M. Overett (b. 1960)

All rights reserved. Without limiting the rights under copyright reserved above, no part of this publication may be reproduced, stored in a retrieval system, or transmitted, in any form or by any means (electronic, mechanical, photocopying, recording or otherwise), without the prior written permission of the copyright owner of this book.

Published by
Lighthouse Christian Publishing
SAN 257-4330
5531 Dufferin Drive
Savage, Minnesota, 55378
United States of America

www.lighthousechristianpublishing.com

Introductory Notice.

The book, On care to be had for the dead, I wrote, having been asked by letter whether it profits any person after death that his body shall be buried at the memorial of any Saint. The book begins thus: Long time unto your Holiness, my venerable fellow bishop Paulinus.

1. Long time, my venerable fellow-bishop Paulinus, have I been thy Holiness's debtor for an answer; even since thou wrote to me by them of the household of our most religious daughter Flora, asking of me whether it profit any man after death that his body is buried at the memorial of some Saint. This, namely, had the said widow begged of thee for her son deceased in those parts, and thou has written her an answer, consoling her, and announcing to her concerning the body of the faithful young man Cynegius, that the thing which she with motherly and pious affection desired was done, to wit, by placing it in the basilica of most blessed Felix the Confessor. Upon which occasion it came to pass, that by the same bearers of thy letter thou didst write also to me, raising the like question, and craving that I would answer what I thought of this matter, at the same time not forbearing to say what are thine own sentiments. For thou sayes that to thy thinking these be no empty motions of religious and faithful minds, which take this care for their deceased friends. Thou adds, moreover, that it cannot be void of effect that the whole Church is wont to supplicate for the departed: so that hence it may be further conjectured that it doth profit a person after death, if by the faith of his friends for the interment of his body such a spot be provided wherein may be apparent the aid, likewise in this way sought, of the Saints.

2. But this being the case, how to this opinion that should not be contrary which the Apostle says, "For we shall all stand before the judgment-seat of Christ, that each may receive according to the things he hath done by the body, whether good or bad;" this, thou signifies, thou dost not well see. For this apostolic sentence doth before

death admonish to be done, that which may profit after death; not then, first, when there is to be now a receiving of that which a person shall have done before death. True, but this question is thus solved, namely, that there is a certain kind of life by which is acquired, while one lives in this body, that it should be possible for these things to be of some help to the departed; and, consequently, it is "according to the things done by the body," that they are aided by the things which shall, after they have left the body, be religiously done on their behalf. For there are whom these things aid nothing at all, namely, when they are done either for persons whose merits are so evil, that neither by such things are they worthy to be aided; or for persons whose merits are so good, that of such things they have no need as aids. Of the kind of life, therefore, which each hath led by the body, doth it come, that these things profit or profit not, whatever are piously done on his behalf when he has left the body. For touching merit whereby these things profit, if none have been gotten in this life, it is in vain sought after this life. So it comes to pass as well that not unmeaningly doth the Church, or care of friends, bestow upon the departed whatever of religion it shall be able; as also that, nevertheless, each received "according to the things which he hath done by the body, whether it be good or bad," the Lord rendering unto each according to his works. For, that this which is bestowed should be capable of profiting him after the body, this was acquired in that life which he hath led in the body.

3. Possibly thy inquiry is satisfied by this my brief reply. But what other considerations move me, to which I think meet to answer, do thou for a short space attend. In

the books of the Maccabees we read of sacrifice offered for the dead. Howbeit even if it were nowhere at all read in the Old Scriptures, not small is the authority, which in this usage is clear, of the whole Church, namely, that in the prayers of the priest which are offered to the Lord God at His altar, the Commendation of the dead hath also its place. But then, whether there be some profit accruing unto the soul of the dead from the place of its body, requires a more careful inquiry. And first, whether it make any difference in causing or increasing of misery after this life to the spirits of men if their bodies be not buried, this must be looked into, not in the light of opinion however commonly received, but rather of the holy writ of our religion. For we are not to credit that, as is read in Maro, the unburied are prohibited from navigating and crossing the infernal stream: because forsooth "To none is giv'n to pass the hideous banks And waters hoarse, ere in their meet abode The bones have sunk to rest." Who can incline a Christian heart to these poetical and fabulous figments, when the Lord Jesus, to the intent that under the hands of their enemies, who should have their bodies in their power, Christians might lie down without a fear, asserts that not a hair of their head shall perish, exhorting that they should not fear them which when they have killed the body have nothing more that they can do? Of which in the first book "On the City of God," I have methinks enough spoken, to break the teeth in their mouths who, in imputing to Christian times the barbarous devastation, especially that which Rome has lately suffered, do cast up to us this also, that Christ did not there come to the succor of His own. To whom when it is answered that the souls of the faithful were, according to the merits of their faith, by Him taken into protection, they insult over us with talking of their corpses left unburied. All this matter, then, concerning burial I have in such words as these expounded.

4. "But" (say I) "in such a slaughter-heap of dead bodies, could they not even be buried? not this, either, doth pious faith too greatly dread, holding that which is foretold that not even consuming beasts will be a hindrance to the rising again of bodies of which not a hair of the head shall perish. Nor in any wise would Truth say, "Fear not them which kill the body, but cannot kill the soul;" if it could at all hinder the life to come whatever enemies might choose to do with the bodies of the slain. Unless haply any is so absurd as to contend that they ought not to be feared before death, lest they kill the body, but ought to be feared after death, lest, having killed the body, they suffer it not to be buried. Is that then false which Christ says, "Who kill the body, and afterwards have no more that they can do," if they have so great things that they can do on dead bodies? Far be the thought, that that should be false which Truth hath said. For the thing said is, that they do somewhat when they kill, because in the body there is feeling while it is in killing, but afterward they have nothing more that they can do because there is no feeling in the body when killed. Many bodies, then, of Christians the earth hath not covered: but none of them hath any separated from heaven and earth, the whole of which He filled with presence of Himself, Who knows whence to resuscitate that which He created. It is said indeed in the Psalm, "The dead bodies of thy servants have they given for meat unto the fowls of the heaven, the flesh of thy saints unto the beasts of the earth: they have shed their blood like water

round about Jerusalem, and there was no man to bury them:" but more to heighten the cruelty of them who did these things, not to the infelicity of them who suffered them. For, however, in sight of men these things may seem hard and dire, yet "precious in the sight of the Lord is the death of His saints." So, then, all these things, care of funeral, bestowal in sepulture, pomp of obsequies, are more for comfort of the living, than for help to the dead. If it at all profit the ungodly to have costly sepulture, it shall harm the godly to have vile sepulture or none. Right handsome obsequies in sight of men did that rich man who was clad in purple receive of the crowd of his house folk; but far more handsome did that poor man who was full of sores obtain of the ministry of Angels; who bore him not out into a marble tomb, but into Abraham's bosom bore him on high. All this they laugh at, against whom we have undertaken to defend the City of God: but for all that their own philosophers, even, held care of sepulture in contempt; and often whole armies, while dying for their earthly country, cared not where they should after lie, or to what beasts they should become meat; and the poets had leave to say of this matter with applause "though all unurn'd he lie,

His cov'ring is the overarching sky."

How much less ought they to make a vaunting about unburied bodies of Christians, to whom the flesh itself with all its members, re-fashioned, not only from the earth, but even from the other elements, yea, from their most secret windings, where into these evanished corpses have retired, is assured to be in an instant of time rendered back and made entire as at the first, according to His promise?

5. Yet it follows not that the bodies of the departed are to be despised and flung aside, and above all of just and faithful men, which bodies as organs and vessels to all good works their spirit hath holily used. For if a father's garment and ring, and whatever such like, is the dearer to those whom they leave behind, the greater their affection is towards their parents, in no wise are the bodies themselves to be spurned, which truly we wear in more familiar and close conjunction than any of our putting on. For these pertain not to ornament or aid which is applied from without, but to the very nature of man. Whence also the funerals of the just men of old were with dutiful piety cared for, and their obsequies celebrated, and sepulture provided: and themselves while living did touching burial or even translation of their bodies give charge to their sons. Tobias also, to have by burying of the dead obtained favor with God, is by witness of an Angel commended. The Lord Himself also, about to rise on the third day, both preaches, and commends to be preached, the good work of a religious woman, that she poured out a precious ointment over His limbs, and did it for His burial: and they are with praise commemorated in the Gospel, who having received His Body from the cross did carefully and with reverend honor see it wound and laid in the sepulcher. These authorities however do not put us upon thinking that there is in dead bodies any feeling; but rather, that the Providence of God (Who is moreover pleased with such offices of piety) doth charge itself with the bodies also of the dead, this they betoken, to the intent our faith of resurrection might be stayed up thereby. Where also is wholesomely learned, how great

may be the reward for alms which we do unto the living and feeling, if not even that be lost before God, whatever of duty and of diligence is paid to the lifeless members of men. There are indeed also other things, which in speaking of the bestowal or removal of their bodies the holy Patriarchs willed to be understood as spoken by the prophetic Spirit: but this is not the place to treat thoroughly of these things, seeing that sufficed which we have said. But if the lack of those things which are necessary for sustentation of the living, as food and clothing, however heavy affliction attend the lacking, do not break in good men the manly courage of bearing and enduring, nor eradicate piety from the mind, but by exercising make it more fruitful; how much more doth lack of those things which are wont to be applied for care of funerals and bestowal of bodies of the departed, not make them wretched, now that in the hidden abodes of the pious they are at rest! And therefore, when these things have to dead bodies of Christians in that devastation of the great City or of other towns also been lacking, there is neither fault of the living, who could not afford these things, nor pain of the dead who could not feel the same. This is my opinion concerning the ground and reason of sepulture. Which I have therefore from another book of mine transferred to this, because it was easier to rehearse this, than to express the same matter in another way.

6. If this be true, doubtless also the providing for the interment of bodies a place at the Memorials of Saints, is a mark of a good human affection towards the remains of one's friends: since if there be religion in the burying, there cannot but be religion in taking thought where the burying shall be. But while it is desirable there should be

such like solaces of survivors, for the showing forth of their pious mind towards their beloved, I do not see what helps they be to the dead save in this way: that upon recollection of the place in which are deposited the bodies of those whom they love, they should by prayer commend them to those same Saints, who have as patrons taken them into their charge to aid them before the Lord. Which indeed they would be still able to do, even though they were not able to inter them in such places. But then the only reason why the name Memorials or Monuments is given to those sepulchers of the dead which become specially distinguished, is that they recall to memory, and by putting in mind cause us to think of, them who by death are withdrawn from the eyes of the living, that they may not by forgetfulness be also withdrawn from men's hearts. For both the term Memorial most plainly shews this, and Monument is so named from monishing, that is, putting in mind. For which reason the Greeks also call that μνημεῖον which we call a Memorial or Monument: because in their tongue the memory itself, by which we remember, is called μνήμη. When therefore the mind recollects where the body of a very dear friend lies buried, and thereupon there occurs to the thoughts a place rendered venerable by the name of a Martyr, to that same Martyr doth it commend the soul in affection of heartfelt recollection and prayer. And when this affection is exhibited to the departed by faithful men who were most dear to them, there is no doubt that it profits them who while living in the body merited that such things should profit them after this life. But even if some necessity should through absence of all facility not allow bodies to be interred, or in such places interred, yet should there be no pretermitting of supplications for the spirits of the dead: which supplications, that they should be made for all in Christian and catholic fellowship departed, even without mentioning of their names, under a general commemoration, the Church hath charged herself withal; to the intent that they which lack, for these offices, parents or sons or whatever kindred or friends, may have the same afforded unto them by the one pious mother which is common to all. But if there were lack of these supplications, which are made with right faith and piety for the dead, I account that it should not a whit profit their spirits, howsoever in holy places the lifeless bodies should be deposited.

7. When therefore the faithful mother of a faithful son departed desired to have his body deposited in the basilica of a Martyr, forasmuch as she believed that his soul would be aided by the merits of the Martyr, the very believing of this was a sort of supplication, and this profited, if aught profited. And in that she recurs in her thoughts to this same sepulcher, and in her prayers more and more commends her son, the spirit of the departed is aided, not by the place of its dead body, but by that which springs from memory of the place, the living affection of the mother. For at once the thought, who is commended and to whom, doth touch, and that with no unprofitable emotion, the religious mind of her who prays. For also in prayer to God, men do with the members of their bodies that which becometh suppliants, when they bend their knees, when they stretch forth their hands, or even prostrate themselves on the ground, and whatever else they visibly do, albeit their invisible will and heart's intention be known unto God, and He needs not these tokens that any man's mind should be opened unto Him:

only hereby one more excites himself to pray and groan more humbly and more fervently. And I know not how it is, that, while these motions of the body cannot be made but by a motion of the mind preceding, yet by the same being outwardly in visible sort made, that inward invisible one which made them is increased: and thereby the heart's affection which preceded that they might be made, grows because they are made. But still if any be in that way held, or even bound, that he is not able to do these things with his limbs, it does not follow that the inner man does not pray, and before the eyes of God in its most secret chamber, where it hath compunction, cast itself on the ground. So likewise, while it makes very much difference, where a person deposits the body of his dead, while he supplicates for his spirit unto God, because both the affection preceding chose a spot which was holy, and after the body is there deposited the recalling to mind of that holy spot renews and increases the affection which had preceded; yet, though he may not be able in that place which his religious mind did choose to lay in the ground him whom he loves in no wise ought he to cease from necessary supplications in commending of the same. For wheresoever the flesh of the departed may lie or not lie, the spirit requires rest and must get it: for the spirit in its departing from thence took with it the consciousness without which it could make no odds how one exists, whether in a good estate or a bad: and it does not look for aiding of its life from that flesh to which it did itself afford the life which it withdrew in its departing, and is to render back in its returning; since not flesh to spirit, but spirit unto flesh procured merit even of very resurrection, whether it be unto punishment or unto glory that it is to come to life again.

8. We read in the Ecclesiastical History which Eusebius wrote in Greek, and Ruffinus turned into the Latin tongue, of Martyr's bodies in Gaul exposed to dogs, and how the leavings of those dogs and bones of the dead were, even to uttermost consumption, by fire burned up; and the ashes of the same scattered on the river Rhone, lest anything should be left for any sort whatever of memorial. Which thing must be believed to have been to no other end divinely permitted, but that Christians should learn in confessing Christ, while they despise this life, much more to despise sepulture. For this thing, which with savage rage was done to the bodies of Martyrs, if it could any whit hurt them, to impair the blessed resting of their most victorious spirits, would assuredly not have been suffered to be done. In very deed therefore it was declared, that the Lord in saying, "Fear not them which kill the body, and afterward have no more that they can do," did not mean that He would not permit them to do anything to the bodies of His followers when dead; but that whatever they might be permitted to do, nothing should be done that could lessen the Christian felicity of the departed, nothing thereof reach to their consciousness while yet living after death; nothing avail to the detriment, no, not even of the bodies themselves, to diminish aught of their integrity when they should rise again.

9. And yet, by reason of that affection of the human heart, whereby "no man ever hated his own flesh," if men have reason to know that after their death their bodies will lack anything which in each man's nation or country the wonted order of sepulture demanded, it makes them sorrowful as men; and that which after death reached not unto them, they do before death fear for their

bodies: so that we find in the Books of Kings, God by one prophet threatening another prophet who had transgressed His word, that his carcass should not be brought into the sepulcher of his fathers. Which the Scripture hath on this wise: "Thus saith the Lord, Because thou hast been disobedient to the mouth of the Lord, and hast not kept the charge which the Lord thy God commanded thee, and hast returned and eaten bread and drunk water in the place in which He commanded thee not to eat bread, nor drink water, thy carcass shall not be brought into the sepulcher of thy fathers." Now if in considering what account is to be made of this punishment, we go by the Gospel, where we have learned that after the slaying of the body there is no cause to fear lest the lifeless members should suffer anything, it is not even to be called a punishment. But if we consider a man's human affection towards his own flesh, it was possible for him to be frightened or saddened, while living, by that of which he would have no sense when dead: and this was a punishment, because the mind was pained by that thing about to happen to its body, howsoever when it did happen it would feel no pain. To this intent, namely, it pleased the Lord to punish His servant, who not of his own contumacy had spurned to fulfill His command, but by deceit of another's falsehood thought himself to be obeying when he obeyed not. For it is not to be thought that he was killed by the teeth of the beast as one whose soul should be thence snatched away to the torments of hell: seeing that over his very body the same lion which had killed it did keep watch, while moreover the beast on which he rode was left unhurt, and along with that fierce beast did with intrepid presence stand there beside his master's corpse. By which marvelous sign it appeared, that the man of God was, say rather, checked temporally even unto death, than punished after death. Of which matter, the Apostle when on account of certain offenses he had mentioned the sicknesses and deaths of many, says, "For if we would judge ourselves, we should not be judged of the Lord. But when we are judged we are chastened of the Lord, that we may not be condemned with the world." That Prophet, truly, the very man who had beguiled him, did with much respect bury in his own tomb, and took order for his own burying beside his bones: in hope that thereby his own bones might be spared, when, according to the prophecy of that man of God, Josiah king of Judah did in that land disinter the bones of many dead, and with the same bones defile the sacrilegious altars which had been set up for the graven images. For he spared that tomb in which lay the prophet who more than three hundred years before predicted those things, and for his sake neither was the sepulture of him who had seduced him violated. By that affection namely, which causes that no man ever hated his own flesh, this man had taken forethought for his carcass, who had slain with a lie his own soul. By reason then of this, the natural love which every man hath for his own flesh, it was both to the one a punishment to learn that he should not be in the sepulcher of his fathers, and to the other a care to take order beforehand that his own bones should be spared, if he should lie beside him whose sepulcher no man should violate.

10. This affection the Martyrs of Christ contending for the truth did overcome: and it is no marvel that they despised that whereof they should, when death was overpast, have no feeling, when they could not by those tortures, which while alive they did feel, be

overcome. God was able, no doubt, (even as He permitted not the lion when it had slain the Prophet, to touch his body further, and of a slayer made it to be a keeper): He was able, I say, to have kept the slain bodies of His own from the dogs to which they had been flung; He was able in innumerable ways to have deterred the rage of the men themselves, that to burn the carcasses, to scatter the ashes, they should not dare: but it was fit that this experience also should not be lacking to manifold variety of temptations, lest the fortitude of confession which would not for the saving of the life of the body give way to the savageness of persecution, should be tremblingly anxious for the honor of a sepulcher: in a word, lest faith of resurrection should dread the consuming of the body. It was fit then, that even these things should be permitted, in order that, even after these examples of so great horror, the Martyrs, fervent in confession of Christ, should become witnesses of this truth also, in which they had learned that they by whom their bodies should be slain had after that no more that they could do. Because, whatever they should do to dead bodies, they would after all do nothing, seeing that in flesh devoid of all life, neither was it possible for him to feel aught who had thence departed, nor for Him to lose aught thereof, Who created the same. But while these things were doing to the bodies of the slain, albeit the Martyrs, not frightened by them, did with great fortitude suffer, yet among the brethren was there exceeding sorrow, because there was given them no means of paying the last honors to the remains of the Saints, neither secretly to withdraw any part thereof, (as the same history testifies,) did the watching of cruel sentinels permit. So, while those which had been slain, in the tearing asunder of their limbs, in the burning up of their bones, in the dispersion of their ashes, could feel no misery; yet these who had nothing of them that they could bury, did suffer torture of exceeding grief in pitying them; because what those did in no sort feel, these in some sort did feel for them, and where was henceforth for those no more suffering, yet these did in woeful compassion suffer for them.

11. Regarding that woeful compassion which I have mentioned, are those praised, and by king David blessed, who to the dry bones of Saul and Jonathan afforded mercy of sepulture. But yet what mercy is that, which is afforded to them that have feeling of nothing? Or haply is this to be challenged back to that conceit of an infernal river which men unburied were not able to pass over? Far be this from the faith of Christians: else hath it gone most ill with so great a multitude of Martyrs, for whom there could be no burying of their bodies, and Truth did cheat them when It said, "Fear not them which kill the body, and after that have no more that they can do," if these have been able to do to them so great evils, by which they were hindered to pass over to the places which they longed for. But, because this without all doubt is most false, and it neither any whit hurts the faithful to have their bodies denied sepulture, nor any whit the giving of sepulture unto infidels advantaged them; why then are those who buried Saul and his son said to have done mercy, and for this are blessed by that godly king, but because it is a good affection with which the hearts of the pitiful are touched, when they grieve for that in the dead bodies of other men, which, by that affection through which no man ever hated his own flesh, they would not have done after their own death to their own

bodies; and what they would have done by them when they shall have no more feeling, that they take care to do by others now having no feeling while themselves have yet feeling?

12. Stories are told of certain appearances or visions, which may seem to bring into this discussion a question which should not be slighted. It is said, namely, that dead men have at times either in dreams or in some other way appeared to the living who knew not where their bodies lay unburied, and have pointed out to them the place, and admonished that the sepulture which was lacking should be afforded them. These things if we shall answer to be false, we shall be thought impudently to contradict the writings of certain faithful men, and the senses of them who assure us that such things have happened to themselves. But it is to be answered, that it does not follow that we are to account the dead to have sense of these things, because they appear in dreams to say or indicate or ask this. For living men do also appear ofttimes to the living as they sleep, while they themselves know not that they do appear; and they are told by them, what they dreamed, namely, that in their dream the speakers saw them doing or saying something. Then if it may be that a person in a dream should see me indicating to him something that has happened or even foretelling something about to happen, while I am perfectly unwitting of the thing and altogether regardless not only what he dreams, but whether he is awake while I am asleep, or he asleep while I am awake, or whether at one and the same time we are both awake or asleep, at what time he has the dream in which he sees me: what marvel if the dead be unconscious and insensible of these things,

and, for all that, are seen by the living in their dreams, and say something which those on awaking find to be true? By angelical operations, then, I should think it is effected, whether permitted from above, or commanded, that they seem in dreams to say something about burying of their bodies, when they whose the bodies are utterly unconscious of it. Now this is sometimes serviceably done; whether for some sort of solace to the survivors, to whom pertain those dead whose likenesses appear to them as they dream; or whether that by these admonitions the human race may be made to have regard to humanity of sepulture, which, allow that it be no help to the departed, yet is there culpable irreligiousness in slighting of it. Sometimes however, by fallacious visions, men are cast into great errors, who deserve to suffer this. As, if one should see in a dream, what Æneas by poetic falsity is told to have seen in the world beneath: and there should appear to him the likeness of some unburied man, which should speak such words as Palinurus is said to have spoken to him; and when he awakes, he should find the body in that place where he heard say while dreaming, that it lay unburied, and was admonished and asked to bury it when found; and because he finds this to be true, should believe that the dead are buried on purpose that their souls may pass to places from which he dreamed that the souls of men unburied are by an infernal law prohibited: does he not, in believing all this, exceedingly swerve from the path of truth?

13. Such, however, is human infirmity, that when in a dream a person shall see a dead man, he thinks it is the soul that he sees: but when he shall in like manner dream of a living man, he has no doubt that it is not a soul

nor a body, but the likeness of a man that has appeared to him: just as if it were not possible in regard of dead men, in the same sort unconscious of it, that it should not be their souls, but their likenesses that appear to the sleepers. Of a surety, when we were at Milan, we heard tell of a certain person of whom was demanded payment of a debt, with production of his deceased father's acknowledgment, which debt unknown to the son the father had paid, whereupon the man began to be very sorrowful, and to marvel that his father while dying did not tell him what he owed when he also made his will. Then in this exceeding anxiousness of his, his said father appeared to him in a dream, and made known to him where was the counter acknowledgment by which that acknowledgment was cancelled. Which when the young man had found and showed, he not only rebutted the wrongful claim of a false debt, but also got back his father's note of hand which the father had not got back when the money was paid. Here then the soul of a man is supposed to have had care for his son, and to have come to him in his sleep, that, teaching him what he did not know, he might relieve him of a great trouble. But about the very same time as we heard this, it chanced at Carthage that the rhetorician Eulogius, who had been my disciple in that art, being (as he himself, after our return to Africa, told us the story) in course of lecturing to his disciples on Cicero's rhetorical books, as he looked over the portion of reading which he was to deliver on the following day, fell upon a certain passage, and not being able to understand it, was scarce able to sleep for the trouble of his mind: in which night, as he dreamed, I expounded to him that which he did not understand; nay, not I, but my likeness, while I was unconscious of the thing, and far away beyond the sea, it might be, doing, or it might be dreaming, some other thing, and not in the least caring for his cares. In what way these things come about, I know not: but in what way soever they come, why do we not believe it comes in the same way for a person in a dream to see a dead man, as it comes that he sees a living man? both, no doubt, neither knowing nor caring who, or where, or when, dreams of their images.

14. Like dreams, moreover, are also some visions of persons awake, who have had their senses troubled, such as phrenetic persons, or those who are mad in any way: for they too talk to themselves just as though they were speaking to people verily present, and as well with absent as with present, whose images they perceive, whether persons living or dead. But just as they which live, are unconscious that they are seen of them and talk with them; for indeed they are not really themselves present, or themselves make speeches, but through troubled senses, these persons are wrought upon by suchlike imaginary visions; just so they also who have departed this life, to persons thus affected appear as present, while they be absent, and whether any man sees them in regard of their image, are themselves utterly unconscious.

15. Similar to this is also that condition when persons, with their senses more profoundedly in abeyance than is the case in sleep, are occupied with the like visions. For to them also appear images of quick and dead; but then, when they return to their senses, whatever dead they say they have seen are thought to have been verily with them: and they who hear these things pay no

heed to the circumstance that there were seen in like manner the images of certain living persons, absent and unconscious. A certain man by name Curma, of the municipal town of Tullium, which is hard by Hippo, a poor member of the Curia, scarcely competent to serve the office of a duumvir of that place, and a mere rustic, being ill, and all his senses entranced, lay all but dead for several days: a very slight breathing in his nostrils, which on applying the hand was just felt, and barely betokened that he lived, was all that kept him from being buried for dead. Not a limb did he stir, nothing did he take in the way of sustenance, neither in the eyes nor in any other bodily sense was he sensible of any annoyance that impinged upon them. Yet he was seeing many things like as in a dream, which, when at last after a great many days he woke up, he told that he had seen. And first, presently after he opened his eyes, Let someone go, said he, to the house of Curma the smith, and see what is doing there. And when someone had gone thither, the smith was found to have died in that moment that the other had come back to his senses, and, it might almost be said, revived from death. Then, as those who stood by eagerly listened, he told them how the other had been ordered to be had up, when he himself was dismissed; and that he had heard it said in that place from which he had returned, that it was not Curma of the Curia, but Curma the smith who had been ordered to be fetched to that place of the dead. Well, in these dream-like visions of his, among those deceased persons whom he saw handled according to the diversity of their merits, he recognized also some whom he had known when alive. That they were the very persons themselves I might perchance have believed, had he not in the course of this seeming dream of his seen also some who are alive even to this present time, namely, some clerks of his district, by whose presbyter there he was told to be baptized at Hippo by me, which thing he said had also taken place. So then he had seen a presbyter, clerks, myself, persons, to wit, not yet dead, in this vision in which he afterwards also saw dead persons. Why may he not be thought to have seen these last in the same way as he saw us? that is, both the one sort, and the other, absent and unconscious, and consequently not the persons themselves, but similitudes of them just as of the places? He saw, namely, both a plot of ground where was that presbyter with the clerks, and Hippo where he was by me seemingly baptized: in which spots assuredly he was not, when he seemed to himself to be there. For what was at that time going on there, he knew not: which, without doubt, he would have known if he had verily been there. The sights beheld, therefore, were those which are not presented in the things themselves as they are, but shadowed forth in a sort of images of the things. In fine, after much that he saw, he narrated how he had, moreover, been led into Paradise, and how it was there said to him, when he was thence dismissed to return to his own family, "Go, be baptized, if thou wilt be in this place of the blessed." Thereupon, being admonished to be baptized by me, he said it was done already. He who was talking with him replied, "Go, be truly baptized; for that thou didst but see in the vision." After this he recovered, went his way to Hippo. Easter was now approaching, he gave his name among the other Competents, alike with very many unknown to us; nor did he care to make known the vision to me or to any of our people. He was baptized, at the close of the holy days he returned to his own place. After the space of two years or more, I learned the whole matter; first, through a certain friend of mine and his at my own table, while we were talking about some such matters: then I took it up, and made the man in his own person tell me the story, in the presence of some honest townsmen of his attesting the same, both concerning his marvelous illness, how he lay all but dead for many days, and about that other Curma the smith, what I have mentioned above, and about all these matters; which, while he was telling me, they recalled to mind, and assured me, that they had also at that time heard them from his lips. Wherefore, just as he saw his own baptism, and myself, and Hippo, and the basilica, and the baptistery, not in the very realities, but in a sort of similitudes of the things; and so likewise certain other living persons, without consciousness on the part of the same living persons: then why not just so those dead persons also, without consciousness on the part of the same dead persons?

16. Why should we not believe these to be angelic operations through dispensation of the providence of God, Who makes good use of both good things and evil, according to the unsearchable depth of His judgments? whether thereby the minds of mortals be instructed, or whether deceived; whether consoled, or whether terrified: according as unto each one there is to be either a showing of mercy, or a taking of vengeance, by Him to Whom, not without a meaning, the Church doth sing "of mercy and of judgment." Let each, as it shall please him, take what I say. If the souls of the dead took part in the affairs of the living, and if it were their very selves that, when we see them, speak to us in sleep; to say nothing of others, there is my own self, whom my pious mother would no night

fail to visit, that mother who by land and sea followed me that she might live with me. Far be the thought that she should, by a life happier, have been made cruel, to that degree that when anything vexes my heart she should not even console in his sadness the son whom she loved with an only love, whom she never wished to see mournful. But assuredly that which the sacred Psalm sings in our ears, is true; "Because my father and my mother have forsaken me, but the Lord hath taken me up." Then if our parents have forsaken us, how take they part in our cares and affairs? But if parents do not, who else are there of the dead who should know what we are doing, or what we suffer? Isaiah the Prophet says, "For Thou art our Father: because Abraham hath not known us, and Israel is not cognizant of us." If so great Patriarchs were ignorant what was doing towards the People of them begotten, they to whom, believing God, the People itself to spring from their stock was promised; how are the dead mixed up with affairs and doings of the living, either for cognizance or help? How say we that those were favored who deceased ere the evils came which followed hard upon the decease, if also after death they feel whatever things befall in the calamitousness of human life? Or haply do we err in saying this, and in accounting them to be quietly at rest whom the unquiet life of the living makes solicitous? What then is that which to the most godly king Josias God promised as a great benefit, that he should first die, that he might not see the evils which He threatened should come to that place and People? Which words of God are these: "Thus saith the Lord God of Israel: concerning My words which thou hast heard, and didst fear before My face when thou didst hear what I have spoken concerning this place and them which dwell therein, that it should be forsaken and under a curse; and hast rent thy garments, and wept before Me, and I have heard thee, saith the Lord of Sabaoth: not so; behold, I will add thee unto thy fathers, and thou shalt be added unto them in peace; and thine eyes shall not see all the evils which I am bringing upon this place and upon them that dwell therein." He, frightened by God's comminations, had wept, and rent his garments, and is made, by hastening on of his death, to be without care of all future evils, because he should so rest in peace, that all those things he should not see. There then are the spirits of the departed, where they see not whatever things are doing, or events happening, in this life to men. Then how do they see their own graves, or their own bodies, whether they lie cast away, or buried? How do they take part in the misery of the living, when they are either suffering their own evils, if they have contracted such merits; or do rest in peace, as was promised to this Josiah, where they undergo no evils, either by suffering themselves, or by compassionate suffering with others, freed from all evils which by suffering themselves or with others while they lived here they did undergo?

17. Some man may say: "If there be not in the dead any care for the living, how is it that the rich man, who was tormented in hell, asked father Abraham to send Lazarus to his five brothers not as yet dead, and to take course with them, that they should not come themselves also into the same place of torments?" But does it follow, that because the rich man said this, he knew what his brethren were doing, or what they were suffering at that time? Just in that same way had he care for the living, albeit what they were doing he wist not at all, as we have

care for the dead, albeit what they do we confessedly wot not. For if we cared not for the dead, we should not, as we do, supplicate God on their behalf. In fine, Abraham did not send Lazarus, and also answered, that they have here Moses and the Prophets, whom they ought to hear that they might not come to those torments. Where again it occurs to ask, how it was that what was doing here, father Abraham himself wist not, while he knew that Moses and the Prophets are here, that is, their books, by obeying which men should escape the torments of hell: and knew, in short, that rich man to have lived in delights, but the poor man Lazarus to have lived in labors and sorrows? For this also he says to him; "Son, remember that thou in thy lifetime hast received good things, but Lazarus evil things." He knew then these things which had taken place of course among the living, not among the dead. True, but it may be that, not while the things were doing in their lifetime, but after their death, he learned these things, by information of Lazarus: that it be not false which the Prophet saith, "Abraham hath not known us."

18. So then we must confess that the dead indeed do not know what is doing here, but while it is in doing here: afterwards, however, they hear it from those who from hence go to them at their death; not indeed everything, but what things those are allowed to make known who are suffered also to remember these things; and which it is meet for those to hear, whom they inform of the same. It may be also, that from the Angels, who are present in the things which are doing here, the dead do hear somewhat, which for each one of them to hear He judged right to Whom all things are subject. For were there not Angels, who could be present in places both of

quick and dead, the Lord Jesus had not said, "It came to pass also that the poor man died, and was carried by the angels into Abraham's bosom." Therefore, now here, now there, were they able to be, who from hence bore thither whom God willed. It may be also, that the spirits of the dead do learn some things which are doing here, what things it is necessary that they should know, and what persons it is necessary should know the same, not only things past or present, but even future, by the Spirit of God revealing them: like as not all men, but the Prophets while they lived here did know, nor even they all things, but only what things to be revealed to them the providence of God judged meet. Moreover, that some from the dead are sent to the living, as, on the other hand, Paul from the living was rapt into Paradise, divine Scripture doth testify. For Samuel the Prophet, appearing to Saul when living, predicted even what should befall the king: although some think it was not Samuel himself, that could have been by magical arts evoked, but that some spirit, meet for so evil works, did figure his semblance: though the book Ecclesiasticus, which Jesus, son of Sirach, is reputed to have written, and which on account of some resemblance of style is pronounced to be Solomon's, contains in the praise of the Fathers, that Samuel even when dead did prophesy. But if this book be spoken against from the canon of the Hebrews, (because it is not contained therein,) what shall we say of Moses, whom certainly we read both in Deuteronomy to have died, and in the Gospel to have, together with Elias who died not, appeared unto the living?

19. Hence too is solved that question, how is it

that the Martyrs, by the very benefits which are given to them that pray, indicate that they take an interest in the affairs of men, if the dead know not what the quick are doing. For not only by effects of benefits, but in the very beholding of men, it is certain, that the Confessor Felix (whose denizenship among you thou piously lovest) appeared when the barbarians were attacking Nola, as we have heard not by uncertain rumors, but by sure witnesses. But such things are of God exhibited, far otherwise than as the usual order hath itself, unto each kind of creatures apportioned. For it does not follow because water was, when it pleased the Lord, in a moment changed into wine, that we are not to regard the worth and efficacy of water in the proper order of the elements, as distinct from the rarity, or rather singularity, of that divine work: nor because Lazarus rose again, therefore that every dead man rises when he will; or that a lifeless man is raised up by a living, in the same way as a sleeping man by one who is awake. Other be the limits of human things, other the signs of divine virtues: other they be that are naturally, other that be miraculously done: albeit both unto nature God is present that it may be, and unto miracles nature is not lacking. We are not to think then, that to be interested in the affairs of the living is in the power of any departed who please, only because to some men's healing or help the Martyrs be present: but rather we are to understand that it must needs be by a Divine power that the Martyrs are interested in affairs of the living, from the very fact that for the departed to be by their proper nature interested in affairs of the living is impossible.

20. Howbeit it is a question which surpasses the

strength of my understanding, after what manner the Martyrs aid them who by them, it is certain, are helped; whether themselves by themselves be present at the same time in so different places, and by so great distance lying apart one from another, either where their Memorials are, or beside their Memorials, wheresoever they are felt to be present: or whether, while they themselves, in a place congruous with their merits, are removed from all converse with mortals, and yet do in a general sort pray for the needs of their suppliants, (like as we pray for the dead, to whom however we are not present, nor know where they be or what they be doing,) God Almighty, Who is everywhere present, neither bounded in with us nor remote from us, hearing and granting the Martyrs' prayers, doth by angelic ministries everywhere diffused afford to men those solaces, to whom in the misery of this life He sees meet to afford the same, and, touching His Martyrs, doth where He will, when He will, how He will, and chiefest through their Memorials, because this He knows to be expedient for us unto edifying of the faith of Christ for Whose confession they suffered, by marvelous and ineffable power and goodness cause their merits to be had in honor. A matter is this, too high that I should have power to attain unto it, too abstruse that I should be able to search it out; and therefore which of these two be the case, or whether perchance both one and the other be the case, that sometimes these things be done by very presence of the Martyrs, sometimes by Angels taking upon them the person of the Martyrs, I dare not define; rather would I seek this at them who know it. For it is not to be thought that no man knows these things: (not indeed he who thinks he knows, and knows not,) for there be gifts of God, Who bestows on these someone, on those some other, according to the Apostle who says, that "to each one is given the manifestation of the Spirit to profit withal; to one indeed," saith he, "is given by the Spirit discourse of wisdom; to another discourse of science according to the same Spirit; while to another faith in the same Spirit; to another the gift of healings in one Spirit; to one workings of miracles; to one prophecy; to one discerning of spirits; to one kinds of tongues; to one interpretation of discourses. But all these worketh one and the same spirit, dividing to every man severally as He will." Of all these spiritual gifts, which the Apostle hath rehearsed, to whomsoever is given discerning of spirits, the same knows these things as they are meet to be known.

21. Such, we may believe, was that John the Monk, whom the elder Theodosius, the Emperor, consulted concerning the issue of the civil war: seeing he had also the gift of prophecy. For that not each several person has a several one of those gifts, but that one man may have more gifts than one, I make no question. This John, then, when once a certain most religious woman desired to see him, and to obtain this did through her husband make vehement entreaty, refused indeed this request because he had never allowed this to women, but "Go," said he, "tell thy wife, she shall see me this night, but in her sleep." And so it came to pass: and he gave her advice, whatever was meet to be given to a wedded believing woman. And she, on her awaking, made known to her husband that she had seen a man of God, such as he knew him to be, and what she had been told by him. The person who learned this from them, reported it to me, a grave man and a noble, and most worthy to be believed.

But if I myself had seen that holy monk, because (it is said) he was most patient in hearing questions and most wise in answering, I would have sought of him, as touching our question, whether he himself came to that woman in sleep, that is to say, his spirit in the form of his body, just as we dream that we see ourselves in the form of our own body; or whether, while he himself was doing something else, or, if asleep, was dreaming of something else, it was either by an Angel or in some other way that such vision took place in the woman's dream; and that it would so be, as he promised, he himself foreknew by the Spirit of prophecy revealing the same. For if he was himself present to her in her dream, of course it was by miraculous grace that he was enabled so to do, not by nature; and by God's gift, not by faculty of his own. But if, while he was doing some other thing or sleeping and occupied with other sights, the woman saw him in her sleep, then doubtless some such thing took place, as that is which we read in the Acts of the Apostles, where the Lord Jesus speaks to Ananias concerning Saul, and informs him that Saul has seen Ananias coming unto him, while Ananias himself wist not of it. The man of God would make answer to me of these things as the case might be, and then about the Martyrs I should go on to ask of him, whether they be themselves present in dreams, or in whatever other way to those who see them in what shape they will; and above all when the demons in men confess themselves tormented by the Martyrs, and ask them to spare them; or whether these things be wrought through angelic powers, to the honor and commendation of the Saints for men's profit, while those are in supreme rest, and wholly free for other far better sights, apart from us, and praying for us. For it chanced at Milan at (the tomb of) the holy Martyrs Protasius and Gervasius, that Ambrose the bishop, at that time living, being expressly named, in like manner as were the dead whose names they were rehearsing, the demons confessed him and besought him to spare them, he being the while otherwise engaged, and when this was taking place, altogether unwitting of it. Or whether indeed these things are wrought, somewhiles by very presence of the Martyrs, otherwhiles by that of Angels; and whether it be possible, or by what tokens possible, for us to discriminate these two cases; or whether to perceive and to judge of these things none be able, but he which hath that gift through God's Spirit, "dividing unto every man severally as He will:" the same John, methinks, would discourse to me of all these matters, as I should wish; that either by his teaching I might learn, and what I should be told should know to be true and certain; or I should believe what I knew not, upon his telling me what things he knew. But if peradventure he should make answer out of holy Scripture, and say, "Things higher than thou, seek thou not; and things stronger than thou, search thou not; but what the Lord hath commanded thee, of those things bethink thee alway:" this also I should thankfully accept. For it is no small gain if, when any things are obscure and uncertain to us, and we not able to comprehend them, it be at any rate clear and certain that we are not to seek them; and what thing each one wishes to learn, accounting it to be profitable that he should know it, he should learn that it is no harm that he know it not.

22. Which things being so, let us not think that to the dead for whom we have a care, anything reaches save what by sacrifices either of the altar, or of prayers, or of

alms, we solemnly supplicate: although not to all for whom they are done be they profitable, but to them only by whom while they live it is obtained that they should be profitable. But forasmuch as we discern not who these be, it is meet to do them for all regenerate persons, that none of them may be passed by to whom these benefits may and ought to reach. For better it is that these things shall be superfluously done to them whom they neither hinder nor help, than lacking to them whom they help. More diligently however doth each man these things for his own near and dear friends, in order that they may be likewise done unto him by his. But as for the burying of the body, whatever is bestowed on that, is no aid of salvation, but an office of humanity, according to that affection by which "no man ever hated his own flesh." Whence it is fitting that he take what care he is able for the flesh of his neighbor, when he is gone that bare it. And if they do these things who believe not the resurrection of the flesh, how much more are they beholden to do the same who do believe; that so, an office of this kind bestowed upon a body, dead but yet to rise again and to remain to eternity, may also be in some sort a testimony of the same faith? But, that a person is buried at the memorials of the Martyrs, this, I think, so far profits the departed, that while commending him also to the Martyrs' patronage, the affection of supplication on his behalf is increased.

23. Here, to the things thou hast thought meet to inquire of me, thou hast such reply as I have been able to render: which if it be more than enough prolix, thou must excuse this, for it was done through love of holding longer talk with thee. For this book, then, how thy charity

shall receive it, let me, I pray thee, know by a second letter: though doubtless it will be more welcome for its bearer's sake, to wit our brother and fellow-presbyter Candidianus, whom, having been by thy letter made acquainted with him, I have welcomed with all my heart, and am loath to let him depart. For greatly in the charity of Christ hath he by his presence consoled us, and, to say truth, it was at his instance that I have done thy bidding. For with so great businesses is my heart distraught, that had not he by ever and anon putting me in mind not suffered me to forget it, assuredly to thy questioning reply of mind had not been forthcoming.

www.ingramcontent.com/pod-product-compliance
Lightning Source LLC
Chambersburg PA
CBHW052045070526
44584CB00018B/2615